STUDY GUIDE FOR THE BULLETPROOF MISSIONARY

Victor Raj

Study Guide for The Bulletproof Missionary

The incredible story of how Professor Shank Ik Moon found purpose in life.

Victor Raj

Copyright © 2019 by Mission Nation Publishing

All rights reserved. No part of this publication may be reproduced, stored, in a retrieval system, or transmitted in any form or by any means – electronic, mechanical, photocopying, recording or otherwise – without the prior written permission of the publisher.

ISBN 978-0-9992577-1-5

FEBRUARY 2019

Mission Nation Publishing
1795 Leamington Rd
Naples, FL 34109

www.MissionNationPublishig.org

The Author of this Study Guide

Victor Raj is the Buehner-Dusenberg Professor of Missions at Concordia Seminary, St. Louis.

Since 1995 Raj has served as the editor of Lutheran Mission Matters, the journal of the Lutheran Society for Missiology. Before that Raj was a parish pastor in India, taught at Concordia Theological Seminary in Nagercoil before becoming the president of that institution. After coming to America he first served on the faculty of Concordia University in Mequon, Wisconsin as professor of theology before becoming the chairman of that department.

Victor and his wife Annie live in St. Louis, Missouri.

TABLE OF CONTENTS

Introduction

Lesson 1: Home Alone

Lesson 2: Taking A Stand

Lesson 3: Like Father, Like Son

Lesson 4: Boy Becomes A Man

Lesson 5: Chaplain's Boy

Lesson 6: From Korea to Kansas and Beyond

STUDY GUIDE FOR THE BULLET PROOF MISSIONARY

by Keriz Rosado

Study Guide

by

Dr. Victor Raj

Introduction

Scripture speaks directly to each person's life. So we read Scripture to help ourselves see how God guides our ways and unfolds his plan every day, moment by moment. The big picture of our lives may not emerge quickly and clearly. We deal with our lives one step at a time, as the Lord keeps us in step with his Spirit. In all this we believe God has a purpose for our lives.

Biblical stories of people, nations and cultures can help us see how our own story finds parallels which comfort and strengthen us with every step we make into the future. But stories of today's saints can help us, too.

Our goal in this guide is to help you consider your purpose in life, as Korean-born Shang Ik Moon did when God intervened in his life. Through six study sessions. Moon, as the book *Bulletproof Missionary* illustrates, experienced God's presence in his life even before he became a Christian! God had been working mysteriously in his life through circumstances, friends and family—many times—even through strangers – to help a boy from Korea find his true purpose in life. Moon heard more than once the Lord's voice, "Lo, I am with you always, even unto the end of the world," (e.g., P.91).

A bright and intelligent boy from a well-to-do middle-class family, Shang Ik unexpectedly became an orphan, survived the hell of living in a war zone, crossed borders through a frozen river, miraculously safeguarded from the bombshells raining over him. Why had God allowed this? What good might come from it?

Living in a war zone was God's way of preparing and equipping Shang Ik to find the purpose of being alive. In the midst of a horrible war, God introduced Shang Ik to a U.S. military chaplain, Chaplain Eduard Vajda, who became a close friend to Shang Ik. That friendship resulted in Jesus becoming Shang Ik's greatest friend. Touched by the Gospel, the Lord's promise "I am with you always" became more personal and real for the boy. This 'moon' began to shine brightly.

Through the chaplain's assistance, Moon learned English and eventually was helped by the Chaplain to move to the U.S. Saying goodbye to the land and the community that brought up and shaped Moon as a young adult was very hard for the boy. His first stop in the United States was Concordia College in Winfield, Kansas.

From Kansas he prepared to train at Concordia Seminary, St. Louis, following The Lutheran Church–Missouri Synod's system to receive a formal theological education for pastors. There Shang Ik also earned graduate degrees from St. Louis University and Washington University.

Moon's accomplishments and an illustrious career led him to help to establish what we know today as Concordia University, Irvine CA, that—prophetically—had first begun as the "Great Commission College." There, as the first Dean of Concordia, Moon expanded the school's vision to make it a cross-cultural Lutheran center for preparing pastors and missionaries of Christ especially among immigrants in North America and across the globe.

Professor Moon's wish to become a missionary to his homeland had not come true. On the other hand, the Lord had been preparing him to be a courageous missionary in the United States.

God is leading each one of us to venture paths that we may not have thought about. But in His wisdom our Lord leads us to serve Him faithfully and joyfully in spreading His kingdom throughout the world through the various vocations He gives us.

For further study: *Several confessions in the letter Paul wrote to the congregation at Philippi connect very well with missionary Moon's life. The Lord revealed to Paul through other people that he was God's chosen instrument to proclaim His name to Gentiles and emperors. Later, Paul confessed that he understood: before Paul was born, God had set him apart for that purpose. If you will read the short Letter to the Philippians along with The Bulletproof Missionary, you will find it both edifying and an encouragement for us who want to become bold witnesses of our Lord, even when faced with opposition, as we give testimony to our faith before a hostile world.*

Professor Victor Raj

Lesson 1: Home Alone

1. Looking back on his traumatic life and losses, Shang Ik Moon conceived this faith statement (page X of *The Bullet Proof Missionary):* "It has been proven to me personally that death is indeed very imminent, always around us, but if we have any breath at all at any given time, it is because God still intervenes in our lives, and the ultimate example of that is the life and death of Jesus Christ and the resulting redemptive work and our eternal home." Can you identify with this view?

2. Read also Philippians 1:21.

3. Reflect on how you might be able to prepare your own faith statement.

4. Living in a war zone is unthinkable for most of us. War kills people and destroys everything God provides for us for living in community . Have you heard or thought about the trauma people go through as they come face to face with war and/or open conflicts in their communities?

5. During World War II, Shang Ik lived in North Korea with his grandmother while his father was serving as an official in the South Korean government. Moon says, "The emotional burden of separation on a child has lasting effects."

a. Reflect on some of the struggles children face during and after long separations from their parents.

b. What are other walls that separate and divide people from family or from whole communities? Explain.

c. How can we as people of God engage in activities that serve others who are hurting, especially as they feel they are abandoned, left out, and do not belong in the mainstream?

d. Compare: Paul exhorts Christians to "stand firm" without being frightened. Philippians 1:27-30.

6. How might the thought of imminent death affect a person's idea of their purpose in life?

Lesson 2: Taking a Stand

"It is very dangerous to cross the border between the North and the South (Korea) right now. It is possible that you may not be able to leave." **(P. 14)**

1. Shang Ik was told his biological mother had passed away. His father, Chun-Soo remarried and moved to South Korea on account of his job. All this time, Shang Ik had been growing up with his grandmother. Now she too died suddenly, leaving Shang Ik orphaned a second time. Until then, grandmother was his mother, his father and his friend.(P.12) What negative effects we've discussed might have affected this child?

2. Border lines divide countries and nations. If families are split apart because of politics, what might be some ways by which extended families or other supportive communities can help alleviate this challenge?

3. Though distanced from one another for various reasons, most parents do have a deep love for their children. How do we know the depth of the love Chun-Soo had for his son Shang Ik?

4. Shang Ik took a stand to see his father against all odds. Describe how focused Shang Ik was in his determination to meet his father.

5. Estrangement from God is the human predicament since Adam and Eve's Fall into sin. But God has brought us back into His family through His Son Jesus. Shang Ik's journey to his father's place was energized by the community that stood with him as he traveled. How does the Christian community stand together when one member gets hurt or falls into deep trouble?

6. "Come along, my son. Let us go home," is the way Chun–Soo

welcomed his son Shang Ik. In what ways do you (or your group) help others appreciate God's joy in seeing new people come into His kingdom through faith in Jesus Christ as their Savior?

7. Read Romans 8:38-39.

What does Paul tell us here that would inform your purpose in life?

Lesson 3: Like Father Like Son

"I understand now why she wants me to leave. I do wish she had just chosen me, though. Why doesn't anyone ever just choose me?"
P. 46

A new home in a new land. Joining his father in Seoul was like a family reunion for Shang Ik. But when his father died he was forced to leave the house. Moving to his sister's house not everyone was friendly. On the world scene, conflicts of interest among the world's super powers also traumatized Shang Ik. But the twelve-year-old managed to live through the new situation.

1. How did Shang Ik's father care for his son while still holding a very important position with the South Korean government for the country's development?

2. Who stepped in as a second mother to Shang Ik? Describe the role she played in Shang Ik's formation.

3. What was Shang Ik's dream as he was growing up as a stellar student in Seoul?

4. When Shang Ik's father died suddenly of a stroke (P.39), it was now his turn to take care of the family, so he thought. But then his stepmother married another man and left Shang Ik an orphan. And tragically, once again, the invasion of Seoul by the North Korean army took the lives of everyone else in Moon's family.

Do you think Moon would have been justified to believe that life is meaningless and empty, especially when his dear ones left him and he had nowhere else to turn? Where will people find comfort if they do not believe in God? (Read Philippians 2:1-11)

5. Let's say we didn't know the full story of Shang Ik's life and how God worked in it. What kind of hope would you have to share with persons who are powerless, seemingly defeated on all sides, having nowhere to turn?

6. In the middle of the battlefield, when all promises failed, Shang Ik remembered his mother telling him "All of life is but a passage of moments. This moment too will pass. And we will be together again." P.54) In what way might this sentiment speak to the people of God about their purpose in life?

Lesson 4: Boy Becomes a Man

"And, lo, I am with you always, even to the end of the world."

Against all odds, Shang Ik was left alone, running for his life with his infant niece who was barely breathing. Braving the freezing weather on a mountainside with the baby on his back, Shang Ik felt lonely, deserted and wished he could die right there. He wondered, "Who would know if I died right here, right here? Who would care?" (p.90) Then from somewhere he heard the words, " Lo, I am with you always, even to the end of the world." Deep in thought, Shang Ik recalled that he had first heard these words from the mouth of a young boy who was tormented by his classmates because he was a Christian. Shang Ik in fact had come to the boy's rescue. This boy had invited Shang Ik to go to church with him and learn more about Jesus. That was then; the words came now!

1. What are some of the opportunities you have found where God provided opportunity to share His word with others?

2. Has God led you to share His word with friends, so they too

can share the joy we have in Jesus Christ? How did that help? Explain.

3. Can you recall any other stories where children, witnessing to their classmates, brought them to faith later in life? Share.

4. Shang Ik was actually caught in the middle of the war between the North Korean and South Korean soldiers. He

happened to be in the frontline, with an infant in hand! Although full of fear and trembling, he was able to understand that the soldier taking custody of him was with the USA! Once the soldiers learned what high school Shang Ik went to, interrogations turned into conversations. After all, the soldier had gone to the same high school in the township where they once lived.

a. What in Shang Ik's life shows why early childhood education can be such an important aspect of Christian mission and ministry?

b. How does Philippians 3:12-14 apply directly to Shang Ik's story at this point in his life?

5. What purpose does God have towards those who do not yet know Him?

6. How does God's purpose towards the world affect your purpose in life?

Lesson 5: The Chaplain's Boy

"Every time I have told the truth, it went well for me. No use to start lying now. I go to church with my friend. He takes me there." (P. 132)

The soldiers believed Shang Ik when he took the risk to tell the truth and let him live. His brother-in-law Jong-Pil was missing. Shang Ik's sister died in the bombing attack. He was left alone to carry their infant daughter and hope that Jong-Pil's brother Kim would be favorably disposed to receive him and the infant with open arms. That was not to be the case. However, the family agreed to take in Shang Ik as a hired hand to work on their farm. Shang Ik later found his niece dead because of malnutrition and exhaustion. Finally, a year later, Shang Ik had to walk away—an orphan once again.

Shang Ik wandered aimlessly in Suwon looking for a job to sustain himself. He went door to door, shop by shop, trying to find a way to make a living, but to no avail. During the sojourn, Shang Ik ran into a group of boys who were just like him, orphaned and having nowhere else to go. They ate from a dumpster where the American military threw the leftovers. Shang Ik's little knowledge of English did him a favor. He was able to connect with the base and later became friends with chaplain Eduard Vajda.

1. If we see our congregations as missionary outposts, (like this chaplain at the military base, for example), how best are we making use of that opportunity for reaching out and inviting people who are 'not like us' to the household of faith?

2. Explain ways in which we can support missionaries who labor for Christ among the new immigrants in our country.

3. Share your experiences with different ways in which Christians engage the world by serving people outside our church walls.

4. Do you have a prayer list that includes intercessions for chaplains or peace keeping officers, or missionaries by name and their families who serve overseas? How would this shape your purpose in life?

Lesson 6: From Korea to Kansas and Beyond

" For me, I cannot prove that God exists based only on quoting theories like Thomas Aquinas. But I can make the assertion. I know God is alive and that He provides for us." (P. 185)

Chaplain Vajda had been God's instrument for changing Shang Ik's life, setting him on a course to become professor Shang Ik Moon. Vajda saw in this young man the skills and talents God had invested in him early in his troubled life, before they could be identified and put to effective use for the expansion of His kingdom. By God's grace Shang Ik grew in faith, and advanced in knowledge. His labor would have everlasting value for those who came to know him and serve faithfully with Professor Moon in God's kingdom.

1. How can individual Christians care for their friends and neighbors, who are new to the American culture, providing for their safety and security?

2. The United States is a nation of immigrants. How can the

church better serve new immigrants, especially in view of prevailing immigration laws?

3. Shang Ik's favorite verse, "I am with you always," is the concluding line of our Lord's command to go into the whole world and make disciples of <u>all nations </u>(Greek "ethnoi," in English, "ethnic."). The Christian faith can be and is shared across cultures. How is your church doing reaching out to people of different ethnicities, heeding the direction the Lord gave his early disciples?

4. Leadership empowerment is an important aspect of expanding Christian ministry in our generation. Suggest helpful ways for identifying leaders who would be servants of the Gospel.

5. In what ways might Christians in America work to raise up a new generation of capable Christian leaders, leaders from different ethnic groups, like Professor Shang Ik Moon?

6. The life and ministry of Shang Ik Moon is a worthy example of how God opens new doors when we think that all doors are shut. What stands out for you in Moon's life that could help you find purpose in your life?

If you found this book and study guide helpful you will want to see the other biographies of the new missionaries to America. You can find them at:

www.MissionNationPublishing.org

Or write to MissionPublisher@aol.com

Made in the USA
Middletown, DE
05 February 2025